Read Write Inc.
Phonics

Red Ditty   Book 5

Fat frog

Created by Ruth Miskin

Stories by Cynthia Rider

OXFORD
UNIVERSITY PRESS

OXFORD
UNIVERSITY PRESS

Great Clarendon Street, Oxford, OX2 6DP, United Kingdom

Oxford University Press is a department of the University of Oxford. It furthers the University's objective of excellence in research, scholarship, and education by publishing worldwide. Oxford is a registered trade mark of Oxford University Press in the UK and in certain other countries

Series created by Ruth Miskin
Stories by Cynthia Rider
Illustrations by Tim Archbold

The moral rights of the author have been asserted

First published 2017

British Library Cataloguing in Publication Data
Data available

ISBN: 978-0-19-840802-4

10 9 8 7 6 5 4 3 2

Paper used in the production of this book is a natural, recyclable product made from wood grown in sustainable forests. The manufacturing process conforms to the environmental regulations of the country of origin.

Printed in China

Helping your child's learning
with free eBooks, essential
tips and fun activities
www.oxfordowl.co.uk

Contents

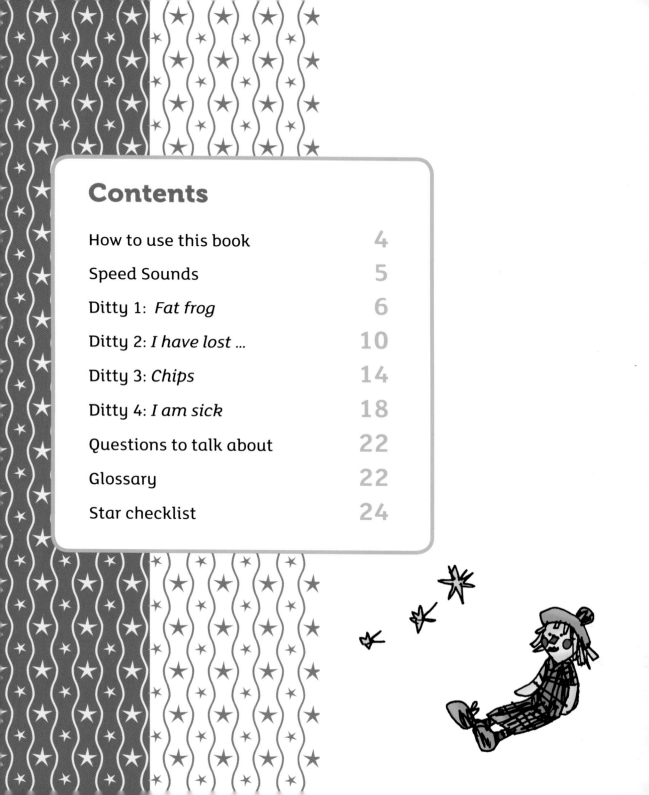

How to use this book

Support your child as they follow each of the steps below. There are notes in italics to guide you throughout the book.

Before reading each ditty, ask your child to read the Speed Sounds on page 5, in and out of order, and then the **Ditty Green Words** and **Ditty Red Words**.

When reading the ditty:

1 Help your child to sound-blend each word (unless your child can already read the word without blending). Praise your child for their effort!

2 Re-read the page to your child and chat about what is happening. (There are questions on pages 22 and 23 to help you.)

3 Encourage your child to re-read the ditty again. Praise your child for reading the words more quickly.

4 Let your child colour in the stars on page 24 as they complete each activity.

Speed Sounds

Each box contains one sound. Sometimes one sound is represented by two letters (a digraph). The digraphs used in this book are circled.

Consonants

Ask your child to say the sounds (not the letter names) in and out of order.

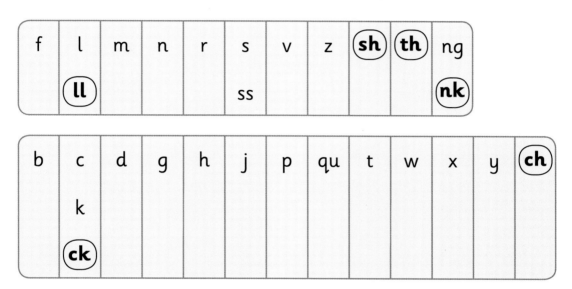

f	l	m	n	r	s	v	z	(sh)	(th)	ng
	(ll)				ss					(nk)

b	c	d	g	h	j	p	qu	t	w	x	y	(ch)
	k											
	(ck)											

Vowels

Ask your child to say the sounds in and out of order.

a	e	i	o	u

Ditty 1 Fat frog

Ditty Green Words

*For each word, ask your child to read the separate sounds (e.g. **f-a-t**) and then blend the sounds together to say the word (e.g. **fat**). Sounds that are represented by more than one letter are underlined.*

a   fat   frog   and   from

ba<u>nk</u>   in   pond   spla<u>sh</u>

Ask your child to read the root word first and then the whole word with the ending.

ki<u>ck</u> → ki<u>ck</u>s   it → its   leg → legs

jump → jumps   land → lands

Ditty Red Words

Red Words don't sound as they look. Read the word out to your child. Ask your child to practise reading the word.

<u>the</u>

Ditty ⭐1

Fat frog

Introduction

This is a ditty about a frog making a splash.

a fat frog kicks
its legs

and jumps from the bank

it lands in the pond

splash!

Questions to ask your child about each ditty are on pages 22–23.

Ditty 2 I have lost …

Ditty Green Words

*For each word, ask your child to read the separate sounds (e.g. **l-o-s-t**) and then blend the sounds together to say the word (e.g. **lost**). Sounds that are represented by more than one letter are underlined.*

> ha<u>ve</u> lost a tru<u>ck</u> do<u>ll</u>
>
> and pen not ted

Ditty Red Words

Red Words don't sound as they look. Read the words out to your child. Ask your child to practise reading the words.

> I my

Ditty 2

I have lost ...

Introduction

This is a ditty about a girl who loses her toys ...

I have lost a truck

I have lost a doll and
a pen

I have not lost my ted

Questions to ask your child about each ditty are on pages 22–23.

Ditty 3 Chips

Ditty Green Words

*For each word, ask your child to read the separate sounds (e.g. **c-a-n**) and then blend the sounds together to say the word (e.g. **can**).*
Sounds that are represented by more than one letter are underlined.

can   ha<u>ve</u>   pop

Ask your child to read the root word first and then the whole word with the ending.

<u>ch</u>ip → <u>ch</u>ips   crisp → crisps

Ditty Red Words

Red Words don't sound as they look. Read the words out to your child. Ask your child to practise reading the words.

no   I   oh

Ditty ⭐3
Chips

Introduction
This is a ditty about a boy who wants to eat chips.

can I have chips

no

can I have pop

no

can I have crisps

no
oh, Mum

Questions to ask your child about each ditty are on pages 22–23.

Ditty 4 **I am sick**

Ditty Green Words

*For each word, ask your child to read the separate sounds (e.g. **b-e-d**) and then blend the sounds together to say the word (e.g. **bed**). Sounds that are represented by more than one letter are underlined.*

am	in	bed	ha<u>ve</u>	got
on	<u>ch</u>in	ne<u>ck</u>	and	
tum	si<u>ck</u>	get	mum	

Ask your child to read the root word first and then the whole word with the ending.

spot → spots

Ditty Red Words

Red Words don't sound as they look. Read the words out to your child. Ask your child to practise reading the words.

I my

Ditty 4

I am sick

Introduction

*Have you ever felt poorly? This is a ditty about a little
girl who is covered in spots.*

I am in bed

I have got spots on my chin, on my neck and on my tum

I am sick
get my mum

Questions to ask your child about each ditty are on pages 22–23.

Questions to talk about

Read the questions aloud to your child and ask them to find the answers on the relevant pages. Do not ask your child to read the questions – the words are harder than they can read at the moment.

Ditty 1: Fat frog

✦ What does the frog do in the ditty? (pages 7 and 8)

✦ What happens to the duck? (page 9)

✦ What noise does the frog make when it lands in the pond? (page 9)

Ditty 2: I have lost ...

✦ What three things has the girl lost? (pages 11 and 12)

✦ Is she happy or sad at the end of the ditty? Why? (page 13)

✦ Have you ever lost a toy?

Glossary

Digraph a single sound that is represented by two letters, e.g. *sh*

Green Words words that your child will be able to read once they have learnt the Speed Sounds in that word

Red Words words that do not sound as they look, e.g. *the, said*

Ditty 3: Chips

★ What three things does the boy want to have? (pages 15–17)

★ What does his mum say? (pages 15–17)

★ What is your favourite food or drink?

Ditty 4: I am sick

★ Why is the little girl in bed? (page 20)

★ Where does she have spots? (page 20)

★ What does the little girl want? (page 21)

Root the part of the word that gives the most meaning

Speed Sounds the letters and the sounds that words are made up of (see page 5)

Star checklist

I can read the Speed Sounds.

I can read the Green Words.

I can read the Red Words.

I can read the ditty.

I can answer the questions
about the ditty.